Big Bad BUGS

by Tracey E. Dils

photography by Corel Corporation
design by Michael Petty

To Phillip, one of the cutest little bugs I know!

First printing by Worthington Press 1997.

Published by Worthington Press
801 94th Avenue North, St. Petersburg, Florida 33702

Printed in the United States of America

2   4   6   8   10   9   7   5   3   1

I S B N   0 - 8 7 4 0 6 - 8 4 7 - 9

dragonflies

Meet the BUGS

Imagine a huge, flying, beast-like bug circling overhead. The bug looks as if it is part dragon, part bird. Its huge wings—which are almost as wide as your own arms outstretched—sound like thunder as they flap above your head.

What is this incredible monster? It's actually the relative of this tiny dragonfly! Big bugs like these lived nearly 300 million years ago. Today dragonflies and other bugs are a lot smaller, but they are still amazing, creepy crawling creatures.

And you are about to enter their secret world!

head

thorax

six legs

abdomen

sugar maple borer

spider

centipede

What is a BUG?

Most people use the word "bug" to describe any creeping or crawling insect, or insect-like creature. Some bugs are insects. To be an **insect**, a creature must have:

 six legs

 a body that is divided into three parts:
1. a **head**
2. a **thorax**
3. an **abdomen**

Spiders and centipedes and millipedes are also usually called bugs, too, but they are not really insects. They have more than six legs and do not have all three body parts.

Bugs do have one important thing in common. Each of them has a special kind of skeleton. This skeleton is called an **exoskeleton**. The exoskeleton is a hard kind of shell that is actually on the outside of the bug's body.

dead leaf
mantid

praying mantis

Dangerous and Deadly

Gruesome Killers

Very few bugs are dangerous to human beings, but many hunt and kill each other.

The praying mantis sits for hours without moving, waiting for its victim. When a smaller bug comes into sight, the mantis does its deadly work. In a matter of milliseconds, the mantis lashes out with its spiked front legs. As it pulls the bug toward it, the spikes sink deeper and deeper into the exoskeleton of its victim. Then the mantis pierces its victim's neck, cutting its nerve cord in two.

Mantises (also called mantids) don't only eat other bugs. They also attack snakes, mice, frogs, and even small birds. Female mantises are even known to eat their mates.

Jaws!

The male stag beetle has a powerful set of jaws. The jaws are really more like super-long hooks! In some cases, they are almost as long as the stag beetle's body.

The stag beetle doesn't use its jaws to attack its prey. It uses them to attack other stag beetles! Two male stag beetles will often fight vicious battles over their territory. They stand up on their back legs and try to knock each other over. The beetle that is knocked over on its back is almost always the loser. That's because the losing beetle can't turn himself back over. Usually, he's eaten by other bugs— like ants!

stag
beetle

Tiny Vampires

Like all spiders, the garden spider has a gruesome way of eating the bugs that it catches in its web. First it uses its sharp fangs to hold its victim. Then it covers the victim with a special kind of juice. The juice actually dissolves the bug's insides. Then the spider devours its meal—by sucking out the bug's liquid guts!

garden spider eating a fly

Human Beings, BEWARE
The Blood Suckers

Some bugs are dangerous to human beings.

Ticks are bloodsuckers. When they attach themselves to an animal's or human's skin, each one is as small as a tiny bead. As the tick sucks its victim's blood, it swells to the size of a marble or a grape. Ticks carry diseases like Rocky Mountain Spotted Fever and Lyme disease.

One of the *most* dangerous insects is the tiny mosquito. Female mosquitoes attack human beings for one important reason—they need their blood! Female mosquitoes need blood from humans and animals to help their eggs grow.

cluster of
swollen
ticks

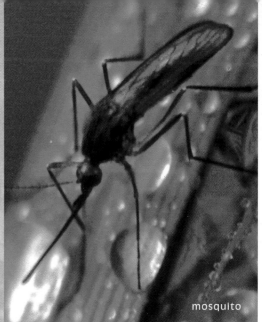

mosquito

The mosquito uses its sharp beak to stab its victim's skin. As she sucks its blood, her saliva enters the victim's body. The saliva is what actually causes the red, itchy bump we call a mosquito bite.

A mosquito bite is usually pretty harmless, but some of the diseases mosquitoes carry are deadly. Yellow fever, malaria, and encephalitis (also known as "sleeping sickness") are just some of the illnesses that can cause death—all because of these tiny pests.

The Stingers

Most bees are peaceful. They seem content to simply fly from flower to flower in search of nectar.

Bees have been known to swarm and attack human beings, though. One species of honey bee from Africa has been labelled "the killer." These killer bees have attacked human beings, dogs, cats, and cows, stinging them until they die.

Scorpions are also deadly stingers. First they grasp their prey with their pincers. If they can't kill their victim that way, they will flip their tail over their head and sting the prey. Scorpions only attack human beings when they are surprised or bothered by them. Their sting contains a powerful poison that can cause serious illness and even sudden death.

bumblebee

giant hairy
scorpion

fireflies

termites

Amazing BUG Tricks

Light Show!

The firefly may look ordinary during the day, but at night, this beetle lights up the sky. A chemical reaction inside the bug's body causes the flashing glow. Lightning bugs light up to communicate with each other. The females have an especially important reason to flash their lights. It's the way that they attract males.

Bug Builders

Termites are incredible builders. They can build towers as high as twenty-six feet. They also like to tear things apart. They eat right through the timbers of wooden buildings and the thick wood of huge trees.

orb web

spider

Bug Weavers

Spiders are the lace makers of the bug world. They weave beautiful webs from the fine silk that their bodies produce. These orb webs probably took the spiders about an hour to build. Each web started with just a single thread between two branches. Then the spider made a Y-shape. Next it wove more threads in a circle, working from the center to the edge.

The silk might look fine and delicate, but it is very strong—deadly strong. It can hold up to 4000 times the spider's weight. And it can mean death for any insect that stumbles into it. The trapped bug will probably become the spider's next meal.

Nature's Singers

Grasshoppers and crickets are known for their special songs, often heard on summer nights. But these bugs aren't actually singing. Grasshoppers make sounds by rubbing their hind legs against their front wings. This insect's large abdomen acts as a kind of drum, making its song even louder. Crickets make their song by rubbing their two front wings together.

The click beetle is not only famous because of the sound it makes. It is an incredible gymnast! When a click beetle is turned over on its back, it does a backflip to right itself. The beetle leans back and then snaps itself over. As it does, it makes a loud clicking sound.

short-horned grasshopper

leaf
katydid

BUG Hide and Seek

A Leafy Disguise

Many bugs use **camouflage**. They look like their
surroundings, which keeps them safe from their enemies.

The leafy katydid can barely be seen as it hides on a green
tree. If it doesn't move at all, it can stay hidden from its
enemies.

The leaf insect uses its leaf-like disguise to blend into its
background. This bug must stay absolutely still or it may
become someone's next meal. When it does need exercise,
it sways back and forth just like a leaf blowing on a tree.

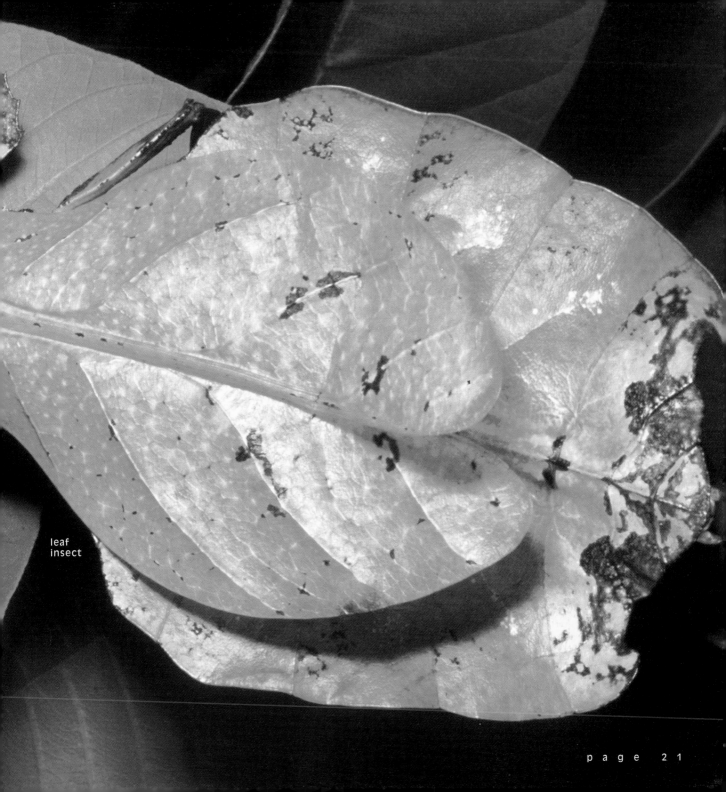

leaf
insect

walkingstick

owl
butterfly

spittle bug

Tricking
the Enemy!

The walkingstick insect looks so
much like a stick that it fools
practically everyone—especially
its enemies. These stick insects
even lay eggs that have their
own form of camouflage.
They look like plant seeds.

The owl butterfly is specially
designed to fool its major
enemies—birds. The round circles
on its wings look like eyes and
these "eyes" confuse the birds
that hunt them for food.

The spittlebug makes its own
hiding place. It blows bubbles
from its back end and hides
in the frothy foam.

Fighting Back!

The blister beetle usually hides itself among bushes. If another creature does try to eat it, it is soon very sorry. The blister beetle squirts out a special liquid that actually causes burns to the skin.

Like a skunk, the stinkbug uses its awful smell to keep enemies away. If it is attacked by a bird or a lizard, it squirts out an awful odor. The smell causes the hunter to lose its appetite in a hurry!

Weaver ants make nests with large leaves to protect their young. They actually sew the leaves together using strands of silk that their bodies produce. If their nest is disturbed, the weaver ants sound a warning by tapping on the leaves from inside the nest. If the intruder doesn't leave, he's sure to be stung. A weaver ant's sting is no ordinary one. These ants squirt acid inside the wound to make it especially painful.

blister beetle

stinkbug

weaver
ants

The Magic of Metamorphosis

monarch
caterpillar

Most bugs change form throughout their lives.
This change is called **metamorphosis**.

All butterflies and moths begin life as a tiny egg. The
moment a caterpillar hatches from the egg, it begins
eating. After about two weeks, it has doubled in size.
Soon, the caterpillar sheds its hard outer skin and forms
a **cocoon**. Inside the cocoon, an amazing change takes
place. The caterpillar transforms itself into a butterfly
or moth. When the magic is complete, the butterfly or
moth emerges. After its wings dry, it begins to fly.

An atlas moth is one of the bug world's largest flyers.
Its wingspan can be as wide as a ruler—twelve inches!

Monarch butterflies are the bug world's long-distance
fliers. They fly about 2500 miles from North America to
Mexico every winter. This is called **migration**. There, they
sun themselves in clusters in the hot Mexican sunshine.
In the summer, they wing their way back home.

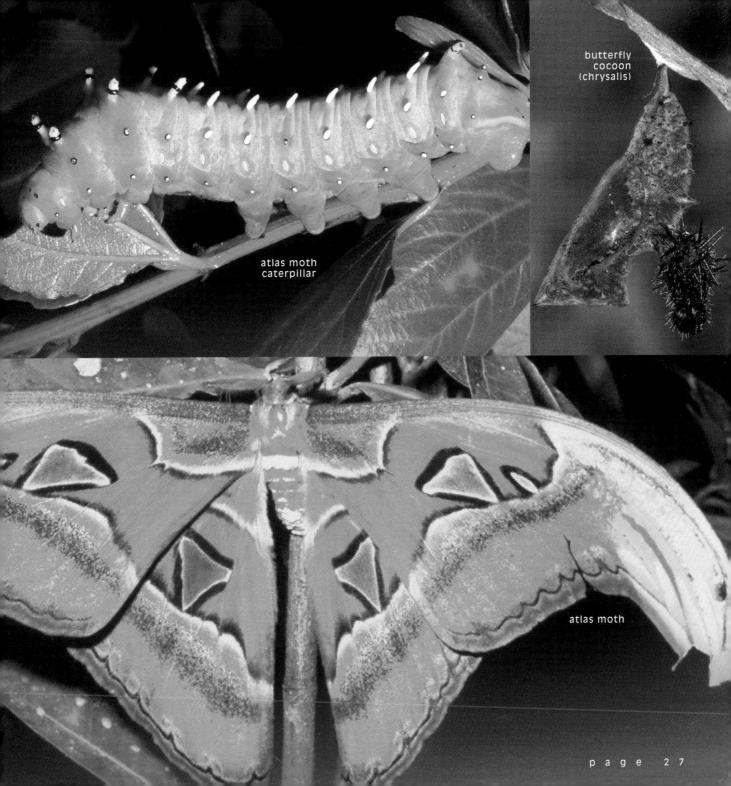

atlas moth
caterpillar

butterfly
cocoon
(chrysalis)

atlas moth

Buried For Seventeen Years!

The cicada spends most if its life underground. When this insect hatches, it is wingless and burrows into the soil, living off the sap from trees.

Cicadas in North America may live like this for about seventeen years. Then they find their way out of the soil. Once on the surface, the cicada's back splits open and the adult winged cicada climbs out. Several thousand others may emerge at about the same time. Together, they climb trees and make weird buzzing sounds that can be heard for long distances. After about six weeks of adulthood, they die off—and their strange song fades along with them.

It's a BUGGY World

thorny
phasmid

Bugs can destroy crops and stored foods, carry diseases, and cause painful bites and stings, but they can also be helpful. Here are some examples of bugs being helpful to humans:

Bees, butterflies, wasps, and hornets **pollinate** plants.

Flies, beetles, and other bugs actually clean up our earth by eating the dead bodies of plants and animals.

Ants and other bugs that live underground add air and other substances to the soil to keep it healthy so that plants can grow.

Bugs provide tasty and nutritious meals for other animals—like birds, fish, frogs, bats, lizards, and monkeys.

Some bugs eat other bugs. Ladybugs, dragonflies, and other insects feast on the bugs that can become pests if their numbers grow out of control.

In some parts of the world, people even eat bugs!

fly

wasp

long-horned beetle

Bugs have been on the earth for a very long time—much longer than human beings have. They have learned to change in order to survive. Bugs are an important part of our world, even if they are a little creepy!

Glossary

ABDOMEN—the last section of an insect's body.

CAMOUFLAGE—the color or markings on an insect or animal that allow it to hide without being seen.

COCOON—the special case made by moths and butterflies to protect themselves as they change form. The technical term for a butterfly cocoon is a chrysalis.

EXOSKELETON—a kind of skeleton that is actually outside the body. The exoskeleton is a hard shell that protects insects and other bugs.

HEAD—the first section of an insect's body. The head may contain six or more eyes, as well as a pair of feelers called antennae.

INSECT—a six-legged bug with three body parts: head, thorax, and abdomen. It changes from an egg to a larvae to an adult by a process called metamorphosis.

METAMORPHOSIS—the way an insect changes from an egg to an adult.

MIGRATION—the seasonal travel of certain insects from one place to another, usually south in the winter and north in the summer.

POLLINATE—the process of transferring pollen from one flower to another in order for seeds and/or fruit to be formed.

SPIDER—an eight-legged creature with two body parts. Most spiders create silk in their bodies and spin webs to catch their prey. Spiders are not insects.

THORAX—the middle section of an insect's body.